neil armstrong

by Annie Laura Smith

The Ardent Writer Press, LLC
Brownsboro, Alabama

If you would like to become an astronaut one day, start by checking out Huntsville, Alabama, and the U.S. Space and Rocket Center.

Visit the **U. S. Space and Rocket Center** at: One Tranquility Base, Huntsville, Alabama.

Be the first in your school to go to Space Camp!

Go to www.SpaceCamp.com

For general information about publishing with The Ardent Writer Press contact *steve@ardentwriterpress.com* or forward mail to: **The Ardent Writer Press, Box 25, Brownsboro, Alabama 35741.**

Neil Armstrong with the X-15 Rocket Aircraft (1960)

Copyright © 2013 by Annie Laura Smith

Published by The Ardent Writer Press, LLC. Jacket Cover by Steve Gierhart, copyright © 2013.

Paperback ISBN: 978-1-938667-09-1

Library of Congress Control Number 2013936864
Library of Congress subject headings:
        Space Shuttle Program (U.S.)--Juvenile literature.
        Children's books--United States--History--20th century.

Photo credits from NASA, the Smithsonian, the Wikimedia Foundation and neilarmstronginfo.com.

Have you ever dreamed of becoming an astronaut?

Astronaut in Space

Neil Armstrong did. He was the first man to walk on the moon.

The Moon

Neil Armstrong was born in Wapakoneta, Ohio, on August 5, 1930, and began his NASA career in his home state.

Neil Armstrong as a child

Neil Armstrong's high school yearbook photo from 1946.

He graduated early from Blume High School, starting college and studying aeronautical engineering at Purdue University in 1947. He earned a master's degree in aerospace engineering from the University of Southern California.

Neil Armstrong took his first ride in an airplane at age six in a Ford trimotor, also known as the *Tin Goose*.

He began taking flying lessons at the country airport near his hometown at age15. He received his pilot's license before he earned his driver's license.

Ford Trimotor Airplane
The *Tin Goose*

Neil Armstrong served as a naval aviator from 1949 to 1952.

During the Korean War, Armstrong flew 78 combat missions in a Grumman F9F-2 Panther, like the one seen here.

His work with the National Advisory Committee for Aeronautics (NACA) led to an assignment with its successor agency, the National Aeronautics and Space Administration (NASA).

He worked as an engineer, test pilot, astronaut, and an administrator for these agencies.

A photo of him as a test pilot with NASA's X-15 Rocket Aircraft is on the credits page.

Neil Armstrong was selected as an astronaut candidate in 1962. He was assigned as command pilot for the Gemini 8 mission.

On this mission Armstrong performed the first successful docking of two vehicles in 1966.

Neil Armstrong in his Gemini Spacesuit

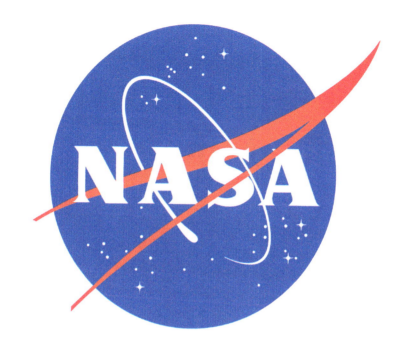

National Aeronautics and Space Administration

NASA Logos

The Story of Apollo 11 and the first man on the

Moon

Neil Armstrong, along with 16 other men, was selected in April, 1967 to support the Apollo Program, NASA's effort to get the first man to the moon.

He was assigned as commander of Apollo 11 in December, 1968.

The Apollo 11 Crew

Neil Armstrong, Mission Commander
Michael Collins, Command Module Pilot
Buzz Aldrin, Lunar Module Pilot

The Mission Patch for Apollo 11 which was worn on the Crew's Flight Suits.

Apollo 11 Launch to the Moon from the
John F. Kennedy Space Center
at Cape Canaveral, Florida
July 16, 1969

Armstrong, Aldrin, and Collins were aboard the command module, *Columbia*, when the journey to the Moon began with the mission launch.

The primary objective was to perform a manned lunar landing and return the mission safely to Earth.

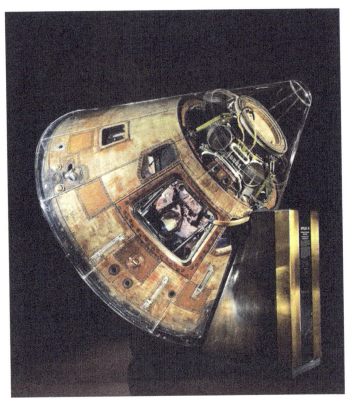

Command Module, *Columbia*, as exhibited at the Smithsonian in Washington D.C.

Neil Armstrong and Buzz Aldrin moved from the command module, *Columbia*, into the lunar module, Eagle. The Eagle landed in the Sea of Tranquility on the surface of the Moon, July 20, 1969.

Michael Collins remained in *Columbia* while Armstrong and Aldrin were on the Moon's surface.

Lunar Module, Eagle as seen leaving the *Columbia*

Earthrise – Photograph of Earth Taken During Apollo 8 Mission Orbit of the Moon

Neil Armstrong Talking to Mission
Control from the Lunar Module, *Eagle*

Neil Armstrong was the first man to step on the surface of the Moon. He did it on July 21, 1969, the day after landing in the crater-marred surface of the moon.

He said, "That's one small step for man, one giant leap for mankind."

Armstrong was the photographer on Apollo 11, so most photographs are of Buzz Aldrin. Here Aldrin steps off the Lunar Module, *Eagle*, to the Surface of the Moon.

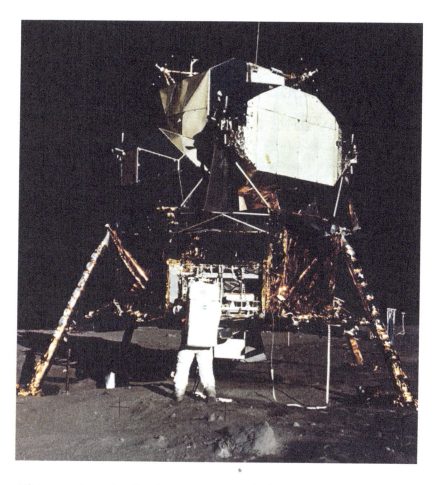

This is what *Eagle*, the Lunar Module, looked like on the moon. The base of the module is still there. Only the top portion of *Eagle* was used to launch Neil Armstrong and Buzz Aldrin back to *Columbia* and Michael Collins.

The astronauts left an American flag and a plaque on the Moon (shown below and on following page).

HERE MEN FROM THE PLANET EARTH
FIRST SET FOOT UPON THE MOON
JULY 1969, A.D.
WE CAME IN PEACE FOR ALL MANKIND

NEIL A. ARMSTRONG
ASTRONAUT

MICHAEL COLLINS
ASTRONAUT

EDWIN E. ALDRIN, JR.
ASTRONAUT

RICHARD NIXON
PRESIDENT, UNITED STATES OF AMERICA

Buzz Aldrin and an American Flag on
the Surface of the Moon

This is an acclaimed photograph of Buzz Aldrin which helped make Neil Armstrong a famous photographer. Armstrong can actually be seen taking the picture. Look on Aldrin's visor and see if you can see Armstrong.

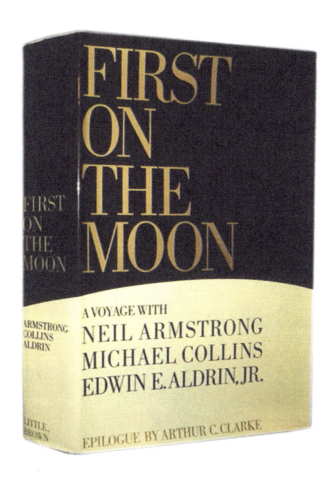

Neil Armstrong wrote a book about the journey to the Moon titled:

First on the Moon: A Voyage with Neil Armstrong, Michael Collins [and] Edwin E. Aldrin, Jr.

Armstrong received international acclaim and many special honors. He was a very humble man, despite his notoriety. The honors flowed as long as he lived, and even after he died.

Here he is shown at a parade in his honor in 1969 at his home town, Wapakoneta, Ohio.

President Bush visits with Neil Armstrong, Michael Collins and Buzz Aldrin, in the Oval Office on July 21, 2004, to commemorate the 35th anniversary of the Apollo 11 mission on the moon.

Among his many awards were the Presidential Medal of Freedom (shown above), the Congressional Space Medal of Honor, and the Congressional Gold Medal.

Neil Armstrong died on August 25, 2012.

The United States Navy will name a new oceanographic research vessel the *RV/Neil Armstrong*. The ship will be launched in 2014, and operated by the Woods Hole Oceanographic Institute.

An asteroid and a crater on the Moon and a new engineering hall at Purdue University were also named after Armstrong.

Neil Armstrong Hall of Engineering
Purdue University
Lafayette, Indiana

Other places named for Neil Armstrong include:

- The county airport in Ohio near his hometown where he took his first flying lessons

- More than a dozen elementary, middle and high schools

- An air and space museum in his hometown

The Neil Armstrong Air and Space Museum
Wapakoneta, Ohio

In Memoriam
Neil Armstrong - Astronaut, Engineer,
Educator and Adventurer
The First Man on the Moon
August 5, 1930 - August 25, 2012

Vocabulary Words and Terms

Apollo Program - The 3rd series of human space flight programs managed by NASA that brought man to the moon. Apollo 17 was the last moonshot (December 1972).

astronaut – person trained to command, pilot, or serve as a crew member of a spacecraft

asteroid – different sized rocky bodies traveling from space

aviator – one who operates an aircraft

crater – a depression in the surface

command module - A Command Module (CM) was the conical crew cabin, designed to carry three astronauts from launch to lunar orbit and back to an Earth ocean landing.

Gemini Program - The 2nd series of NASA manned space flights (1962-1966) that prepared scientists and astronauts for the moon program, Apollo.

launch – to send a missile, space vehicle, satellite, or other object into the air or into space

lunar – relating to the Moon

lunar module - The Lunar Module (LM) was designed to descend from lunar orbit to land two astronauts on the Moon and take them back to orbit to rendezvous with the Command Module.

mission – a journey into space

Mission Control – engineers who control space flights

NASA – National Aeronautics and Space Adminstration

Saturn V - The rocket launch vehicle for the Apollo missions to the moon. For the early orbital flights that did not go to the moon, NASA used a smaller version called Saturn IB.

space – the area between celestial bodies and Earth, exclusive of atmospheres

voyage – a long journey to a distant place

About the Author

Annie Laura Smith has written five historical novels for young readers. She and her son and daughter were at Cape Canaveral on June 18, 1983, and watched *Challenger* launched into space with Sally Ride aboard as the Mission Specialist. Smith lives in Huntsville, Alabama, near the Marshall Space Flight Center. She is the author of an Early Reader biography of Sally Ride, the first woman to go into space.

Lightning Source UK Ltd.
Milton Keynes UK
UKOW06f1830230514

232198UK00010B/60/P